Introduction

When a loved one passes on, the heart begins to ache and your head becomes clouded with memories of he or she, and a loss of words takes place, leaving us in a numb state of mind. You find it hard to accept, but when reality sets in, it's just as hard to deny. You wonder what there is to say about a situation that has come so suddenly without warning. All in all, losing a loved one brings us a feeling of confusion, putting us in shock, sorrow, and in tears, making it hard to search for the right words to say goodbye.

This book is dedicated to all that have lost loved ones and are at a loss for words at their funerals and gravesides

Table of Contents

Last Goodbye

Come with me to the burial sight
To say your last goodbye
Think of me every now and then
Then try to realize
That passing on is not the end
But a means to start again
In a place that's far more peaceful
Then the world we're living in
Let your thoughts convince you
While time keeps ticking on
That we will meet another day
To seal our earthly bond
Keep the faith your heart holds
And try to do your best
So your final conciliation prize
Won't end up in a mess
All your love goes with me
Along with your tears and sighs
I'm wishing you all the very best
While I'm saying my last goodbye

A Temporary Goodbye

The lord whispered to —————
(name)

Take my hand and come with me

There are other friends and loved ones

Who's been waiting patiently

With open arms and greetings

And smiles to welcome you

To a place unknown to mankind

With a love you never knew

The people here will miss you

For the joy you brought to them

But there will be another time

When we will meet again

So ————— went home today
(name)

While we show our sorrow and cry

Remember ————— with a softer heart
(him/her)

It's a temporary goodbye

Go With the Angels

Go with the angels ‾‾‾‾‾‾‾‾
                    (name)
Back where it all began
Take all our love along with you
Until we meet again
Say hello to the loved ones
That came and left before you
Enjoy all the fruits of your labor
In ways that you never knew
Look down upon us now and then
And smile with relief
Knowing we'll be with you
When it's time for us to leave
Let us shed our tears today
And be sad that you are gone
Keeping you in our memories
While we carry on
There's nothing more to say for now
And there's nothing more to do

So go with the angels ‾‾‾‾‾‾‾‾
                       (name)
While we say goodbye to you

Grandpas Goodbye

Oh grandpa, grandpa why did you go
And leave us alone this way
Now we won't see our Santa Claus
When it comes to Christmas day
We knew by your voice that it was you
So we went ahead and played the game
But you were the best of all of them, to use the Santa name
You played ball and told us stories
And you gave us all your love
Now you have left to go and live, in that castle up above
We're going to miss you oh so much
And all that you have done
But when it comes to grandpas, we were the lucky ones
Take our love and rest in peace
It's time to say goodbye, we never will forget you
But for now we want to cry

Grandmas Memory

Today is a sad day for all of us. We lost the one we all loved so much, our grandma. She was always the peace maker with love for both sides. She was always there when one of us became sick. She was always ready to listen to any or all of our troubles and be fair in every way she could. She was always on standby whenever anyone needed help, and when the kids wanted some cookies grandma was there. Grandma raised her family, then when they were grown, she devoted the rest of her days to others. She was well experienced in showing love that would be hard to equal. Grandma will never be gone because she will always be present in our hearts and in our memories. We love you grandma. Rest in peace.

Goodbye To Dad

Dad was the rock of the family
He was strong in every way
He loved ___(me/us)___ with his great big heart
With a love ___(I/we)___ never repay

His protection couldn't be better
His decisions were always fare
And there wasn't anything that dad had
That he wouldn't let you share

He worked hard to support all ___(my/our)___ needs
He was one who never complained
And the kindness he showed to all of us
Is something ___(I/we)___ can't explain

Dad's view of life was simple
So he treated everyone he met nice
And if he hurt anyone's feelings
You can bet he wouldn't do it twice

So with a sadden heart and a sadden mind
___(I/we)___ say goodbye to dad
But you can be sure ___(I'll/we'll)___ always remember
He was the best father ___(I/we)___ could have ever had

Goodbye to Mom

Mom was $\overline{\text{(my/our)}}$ most precious one

And far beyond compare

With radiance you couldn't ignore

But one you wanted to share

She had a kindness that was hard to forget

With a smile full of love

And when she spoke it was very soft

Like an angel from above

When $\overline{\text{(I/we)}}$ had troubles, they became hers

Until she made things right

But she always kept her temper down

And her heart was always light

There is no way to thank her

Because there's no appropriate words

And there wouldn't be any justice

For all $\overline{\text{(my/our)}}$ mom deserves

$\overline{\text{(I'm/we're)}}$ surely going to miss her

And $\overline{\text{(I'm/we're)}}$ surely going to cry

But she'll never leave $\overline{\text{(my/our)}}$ memory

After this goodbye

$\overline{\text{(I/we)}}$ love you mom with all $\overline{\text{(my/our)}}$ heart(s)

But it's so hard to believe you're gone

So for now there is not much more $\overline{\text{(I/we)}}$ can say

But goodbye mom, goodbye

Goodbye Son

The loss of our son is heavy

And our eyes are already sore from tears

Now we do nothing but wonder

How we can face the future years

He was much more then just our child

Whom we loved beyond compare

Now our hearts are broken without any chance of repair

How do you lose such a treasure

How do you ever respond

When it's almost impossible to say goodbye

Then try to carry on

There are no comforting words to express the way we feel

But we do know that this human sorrow is very, very real

Of course we're going to miss you in every kind of way

You'll be in our hearts forever

But we must say goodbye today

Goodbye Daughter

The loss of our daughter is heavy
And our eyes are already sore from tears
Now we do nothing but wonder how we can face the future years
She was much more then just our child whom we loved beyond compare
Now our hearts are broken without any chance of repair
How do you lose such a treasure
How do you ever respond
When it's almost impossible to say goodbye then try to carry on
There are no comforting words
To express the way we feel
But we do know that this human sorrow is very, very real
Of course we're going to miss you in every kind of way
You'll be in our hearts forever
But we must say goodbye today

Goodbye Big Brother

A big brother is what he was

And ——— was his name
(name)

Now he's gone and left me

With a feeling I can't explain

He was always there to help me

With the things I needed to know

Now going on without him

Will be very hard I know

Respect your elders he always said

That's what you should do

Someday you will be an elder

Wanting respect for you

A big brother like ———
(name)

Was special in every way

And it's for sure I am going to miss him

Each and every day

He gave me his love and shared his time

To show me how much he cared

Now I'm saying my last goodbyes

To a brother whose love I shared

I'm going to miss you ———
(name)
More than you will ever know
But most of all I'm sorry to see
My big brother go

Goodbye Little Brother

He was only (age) years old and he wasn't very tall
But much too young to leave us
When he received his final call
He was my younger brother, a real bundle of joy
Head strong every now and then
For such a young boy
I tried to teach him right from wrong, like older brothers do
So he wouldn't get into trouble
With a crime he couldn't undo
He was a great little brother so I'll miss him in every way
Like the way he used to hug me
And the things he used to say
(Name) was my brother's name, now he's gone away
While I'm shedding many tears now
There will be more to come my way
So goodbye little brother until we meet again
With all the love I have for you
I'm sorry to see it end

Older Sisters Memory

———— was a loved one
(name)

She was so much more then we knew

Open hearted and loving in all that she would do

An older sister in every way and bossy

From time to time

With the sweetest smile that could melt you away

A treasure that was mine

All of us that loved her will miss her beyond compare

And the part of our heart that was broken

Is the part that will never repair

Each day I will take a minute

To give ———— a thought
(name)

Forgetting all the heartaches that her leaving us has
brought

Sometimes I'll smile and sometimes I'll cry

But the tears I shed now and then

Will take a long time to dry

Saying goodbye to a sister is impossible to express

But bringing her memories back again

Puts our minds to rest

So goodbye to you ———— until we meet again
(name)

We love you with all our hearts

The way it's always been

Younger Sister's Memory

——————was a loved one,
(name)

She was so much more then we knew
Open hearted and loving in all that she would do
A younger sister in every way
And a handful from time to time
With the sweetest smile that could melt you away
A treasure that was mine
All of us that loved her will miss her beyond compare
And the part of our heart that was broken
Is the part that will never repair
Each day I will take a minute to give ——————a thought
(name)

Forgetting all the heartaches
That her leaving us has brought
Sometimes I'll smile and sometimes I'll cry
But the tears I shed now and then
Will take a long time to dry
Saying goodbye to a sister is impossible to express
But bringing her memories back again
Puts our minds to rest
So goodbye to you ——————until we meet again
(name)

We love you with all our hearts
The way it's always been

A Friend

_____ was not just a friend
(name)

_____ was far more then we knew
(he/she)

An inspiration in every way

With a loyalty that was true

An encouragement to follow your dreams

A support without any end

Yet a winner in every way

Over and over again

Incredible is putting it lightly

For the person _____ has been
(he/she)

Because the level of bonding that we had

I may never have again

While our sorrow is increasing

With the tears that's falling free

For the loss of such a loved one

Tells us how hard it's going to be

Friendship like _____ doesn't come easy
(his/hers)

And will be missed for a long time

Though ‾‾‾‾‾ is unforgettable
(name)

‾‾‾‾‾ will always be on my mind
(he/she)

So go with all our love my friend

Go to your resting place

You will always be remembered

But never be replaced

Remembering A Loved One

Because we are human we have received the blessing of mortal man, with all the joy and sorrow of life. Yet one of our downfalls is that we only see clearly through our hearts. So when we lose a loved one, it brings out the sorrow part of this blessing. Because what we see through our hearts is how much we loved and how much we are going to miss _____ (name) 's presents and companionship. Yet if _____ (he/she) could, _____ (he/she) would have said "don't let your tears hold you down for I will always be with you". So at this hour, we are shedding our tears while _____ (name) goes to _____ (his/her) resting place.

_____ (name) will always remain in our memories, keeping them around in our hearts. Goodbye _____ (name) , goodbye.

Remembering Her

———— is a loved one
(name)

We must not forget

She was so much more than we knew

Open hearted and unselfish

In all of the things she would do

She wasn't blessed with good health

Pain plagued her every day

But she never complained about it

She simply went about her way

She cared a great deal for her family

Of this you can be sure

With the honor she brought to her marriage

How could anyone ask for more?

Her grandchildren were the stars of her eyes

They filled her with daily pride

Along with her love and caring

Was a glow that ———— couldn't hide
(name)

———— lived her life in a saintly way
(name)

Over and over again

She was a sweet and loving person
And her memory will never end
On the other side she's welcomed
While for her loss we cry
Now she's in a better place
So we must say goodbye

Goodbye (name)

When ‾‾‾‾‾ finished saying his goodbyes, he left all of us
       (name)
here with tears in our eyes. I have pondered with my
thoughts, while searching for a relief from this terrible and
unexplainable feeling, which we all know as grief. I have
come to realize that this emotion in particular is so strong,
it's almost impossible to keep under control. Yes it's true,
the only remedy seems to be time, but when the tragedy of
losing a loved one or someone very close to you strikes,
and then at that moment, time has no importance. While we
are all born filled with tears and sorrows that must be
released periodically throughout life, we are also born with
a trigger that allows all of our control to go out of sink,
leaving us in a numb stat of mind. However, we must
remember that sorrows and tears are ok, and a part of our
nature. It is also important to know that we must carry on,
giving Father Time a chance to help heal. We will never
forget what a great loss ‾‾‾‾‾ is, but at the same time we
                         (name)
will always remember what a magnetic person ‾‾‾‾‾‾ was.
                                             (he/she)
Creating a silent love in the hearts of everyone ‾‾‾‾‾‾ met.
                                                 (he/she)
So let us close our eyes and quietly whisper,
"Goodbye ‾‾‾‾‾ , Goodbye".
          (name)

Parents Thoughts

Oh how I miss the child I have lost
And I find no way to measure the depths of my sadness
Yet deep inside I know that I must carry on
I feel now there is no reason to go on living
While at the same time I realize this isn't true
And while I desperately need help
From the very one I'm tempted to blame
It makes this human confusion seem to grow with every
passing day
Why seems to always be the question
But if the answer is there
Then why again is it so hard to accept
Or is it only being human

A Grieving Mom

A cancer came and took my child
At a very early age
It broke my heart a thousand ways
And put me in a rage

The tears have made my eyes sore
But there's no one I can blame
It makes me want to curse my God
Cause I lost him just the same

He was only seven
When his hair began to fall
I knew this happened to older ones
But he was much too small

It's going to be a challenge
Now that he is gone
So how can I count my blessings
When I feel it's all so wrong

Time after time I will remember
And I will think of the hundreds more
Mom's that will lose their child
And cry till their eyes are sore

Cancer is a terrible killer
And it takes a serious toll
Especially with little children
Along with a mothers soul

It came and took my child
There was nothing I could do
So I'm hoping the God I wanted to curse
Gives me a better view

A Last Memory

She was a loved one we must not forget
She was much, much more then we knew
Unselfish with an open heart
In the things that she would do

She wasn't a very strong one
While pain plagued her every day
But she never complained about it
She simply went about her way

She cared a great deal for her family
Of this you can be sure
And of the honor she brought to her marriage
Who can ask for more

Her grandchildren were the stars in her eyes
That filled her with daily pride
Along with the love and caring
Was a glow that she couldn't hide

She lived her life in a saintly way
Over and over again
She was a sweet and loving person
And her memory will never end

Now she's on her way to a new life
While we show our respects and cry
From the bottom of our hearts
Good-bye, good-bye, good-bye

A Prayer

Walk with me in the shadows
Holding my hand so tight
Help me with all the fears I have
So I may feel alright

Whisper to me so softly
The things that I should know
Like giving a friendly smile
Where ever I may go

Let me shed tears of sorrow
For the bad things I employ
Hoping that you'll forgive me
And turn those tears to joy

Give me more endurance
In every kind of way
To be a better person
With every passing day

Help me with more understanding
And giving all that I can
To show you I am thankful
For the way you gave me your hand

Let my days go by with your blessings
Let there be peace in my mind at the start
All these things I ask for
From the bottom of my heart

Hail to the Grandma's of America

Hail to the Grandmas of America
Bless them for all they do
When the Grandchildren are around
There's a bond of love that is true

Over and over they toil
Doing a job they thought was done
But when their kids had their kids
A new job has just begun

They're the backbone of our country
For taking for taking care of our kids
While their sons and daughters are working
They're redoing what they already did

It's not easy to raise a family
Without doing it twice
But the Grandmas of America
Are making that sacrifice

They're doing it for loves sake
Stronger than we'll ever know
And it's all about the Grandkids
Because they love them so

So Hail to the Grandmas of America
For the hero's they've become
And we love them with all our hearts
For all the good that they have done

Memories

Memories are like connectors
Bringing past events to review
So they can be relived over again
Whether good or bad old or new

The sad ones are too private
For anyone else to share
Bringing back so many tears
To show how much you care

Good ones bring back connectors
Of the years that passed by
While leaving several smiles
And a satisfying sigh

The bad ones bring an anger
You can't get out of your mind
How people do the things they do
With no remorseful sign

The happy ones in general
Are for family folks and friends
So when we're all together
There's laughter without end

Circle of Life

Raindrops tapping on the roof top
Lightning flashing now and then
Darkness all around you
Pondering thoughts are back again

Children playing on the playground
Parties for the teens
Dating with excitement
Wanting to share your dreams

College yes or maybe
Movies and ballets
Vacations in the summer
Plans for future days

Love around the corner
With hope by its side
While plans begin to falter
From feelings you can't hide

Marriage in the making
Childbirth in a year
Struggling to make ends meet
In a different atmosphere

Retirement in the forecast
With several years to go
What happened to the dreams you had
So very long ago

Father time was the culprit
The Circle of Life had a hand
And adulthood, love and family
Became your first command

Yet when it's all over
While it's passing in review
It's a never ending circle
Whatever you do

Life Itself

By Ralph S. O'Brien

Life brings pain and hope along with joy. Our bonds are what hold us together. Family, friends and our sincere attitude in what we believe are all part of the system. So we must realize, understand, and accept all the elements pertaining to this vast and eternal existence in which we are a very small part. It is true there is nothing in life so permanent that a change can't take place to upset the harmony we live in, and leaves us in a depressing state of mind. However, hope always allows us to interfere with these depressed moods and the success that follows is what god gave us, our joys and our sorrows. All in all, the road of life has many ups and downs; in which some we have no control. Therefore, we must have some sort of way to keep a level of balance. That level is determined by our temper, anger, understanding, and solutions. After all, what more do we have?